# An Immigrant's
# guide
# to
# Living in America

A guide from one immigrant to another;

avoid rookie mistakes, hit the ground running...!!!

By

**Shola Agbebi, MBA**

# Preface

This book is inspired by my personal experience of living in the United states of America (commonly referred to as America, and/or USA) as a legal immigrant from Nigeria. This book basically is a guide to living in America, written by an "experienced" immigrant to a "newcomer" or "rookie" immigrant. the book gives you a comprehensive basic knowledge of America, and of living in America. By the time you are done with this book, you would have learned some basic but very important things about America and found some new confidence living in your new country.

This book serves a guide to people coming to America as immigrants (permanent residents), and non-immigrants planning to stay for an extended period, for example, students. It can also be utilized by illegal immigrants, (I probably shouldn't say that, but it's true, that's the reality we live in now), however the target audience for this guide are legal immigrants to the USA. In addition, this guide would make an interesting read for other "experienced" immigrants, green card holders, and to all citizens of the USA.

When I came to the USA, now my home, nobody gave me a comprehensive guide, I wish I had some guidance. What I had were tit bits, hearsays, myths, half-hearted advices, and basically had to live and learn from experience (which is the best teacher). Failing, falling, making mistakes, picking myself up, correcting myself, and through self-motivation, and self-education, now I am "soaring on wings like the eagle". Glory to God Almighty! Can I just say here, that falling, or failing is not a problem; it is what you do after falling that may result into a problem or result into a sure path toward success. Word!!

This book (or guide) reflects my personality; down to earth, humble, no hype, straight shooting, honest, humorous, bold, and full of courage, among other winning qualities. Lol.

The contents of this book are sincere, and I don't wish you to make mistakes others made (including my humble self) and trust me they can be costly. You don't have to make these same mistakes, so my sincere wish is that the contents of this book will help jumpstart your new life in America, and help you make the right decisions, the first time, all the time.

I pray and hope you find this book very useful.

May God bless you, and may God bless America, Amen.

Good luck, my friend. Enjoy!!!

# DEDICATION

This book is dedicated to God Almighty, Jehovah El-Shaddai, King of kings and Lord of lords, the creator of heaven and earth, and of the whole universe and of everything in it.

The I am that I am.

To Him alone be the kingdom, the power, and the glory, all thanks, and adoration;

forever & ever, Amen.

# Contents

# Coming to America

The first step towards coming to America is applying for a visa, either an immigrant or a non-immigrant visa. Some citizens of certain countries do not require a visa to come to the USA, these countries participate in the US visa waiver program. Under this program, citizens of these countries can come to the USA, and stay for 90 days without a visa, these countries include:

*Andorra, Australia, Austria, Belgium, Brunei, Chile, Czech Republic, Denmark, Estonia, Finland, France, Germany, Greece, Hungary, Iceland, Ireland, Italy, Japan, Republic of Korea, Latvia, Liechtenstein, Lithuania, Luxembourg, Malta, Monaco, Netherlands, New Zealand, Norway, Portugal, San Marino, Singapore, Slovakia, Slovenia, Spain, Sweden, Switzerland, Taiwan, and the United Kingdom*

However, citizens from other countries not listed here do need a visa. There are a variety of non-immigrant visas, the more common non-immigrant visas are the visitor/tourist, business, work, or student visa.

No matter which country you are coming from, all requirements for applying for a visa can be obtained from the official website of the United States department of homeland security.

After applying for a visa online and meeting all the requirements stated as it relates to you, you'll schedule an interview and physically visit the US embassy or consulate in your country for the interview. From my experience, the interviewing officer basically wants to find out 3 things:

1. If you plan to come back to your country after your visit to the USA
2. If you are going to be a responsible visitor (financially, law abiding, etc.)
3. If you are going to be a security risk to the USA

So, my advice is, be honest, sincere, and confident in your answers, and provide supporting documents where needed.

Two things will happen after the interview, either:

1:    You are denied a visa with instructions on your next course of action. You may appeal the decision or reapply after a couple of months.

2:    You are issued a visa. Congratulations! start making plans to come to America.

# Welcome to America

Now you have arrived at the United States of America, let me welcome you into America. A word of advice, on or before your visa expires please go back to your country. Life here as an illegal immigrant is miserable, some people come into the USA with a visitor or student visa, and allow the visa to expire without returning to their countries, now they are illegal, and without the proper documentations, they can't work legally, they are financially broke, they move around scared of the authorities, some people take advantage of them and abuse them physically and mentally. Now, if they get deported, or leave the United States, chances of being issued another visa is almost zero. They are stuck in a rot. Don't let that be you. Please reside here legally!!

As a legal immigrant, hopefully you have come to live in America as a responsible resident, may your days and years here be prosperous. You emigrated from your country of origin to live in America. People come from all over the world to live in USA for a variety of reasons. The top reason being that USA is one of the greatest countries in the world today, if not the greatest, and provides ample opportunity and protection to live out your dreams. Please don't take this opportunity lightly. Do not abuse it but take advantage of it. These opportunities include jobs, security, education, health, housing, economic infrastructures, and business opportunities. These translate to a higher standard of living, available in a few other countries in our world today. The greatest gift of America is freedom: freedom of speech, of religion, of expression; freedom to express yourself and live life within the limits of the law.

Living in America can come as a huge culture shock, or an experience of a huge cultural difference from the one you are used to back in your country, especially if you're from Africa, Asia, the middle east, even from Europe, pretty much from everywhere, so be prepared for the "shock". Luckily, you've got this book to guide you at least. Yaay!!

Now you're in America, there are a couple of things you need to know and do as a matter of urgency.

1. Get your Social security number (SSN), SSN card, and a government identification card, preferably a driver's license from the state where you're resident, for example a Georgia State driver license, or a Texas driver license, every state issues its own state driver's license.

   You can procure your SSN and card from any of the Social security administration offices located in your state of residence, and your driver's license from the department of motor vehicles (DMV), like I said earlier, every state in the United State has a DMV, where driver licenses, plate/tag numbers, car title, etc. are issued. When you are ready to visit these offices, book an early morning appointment and arrive early, so you can leave early.

   The SSN is very important, it is your identity in America, everything you will ever do in this country is tied to your SSN, and credit bureau profile (We'll get to that later). However, regarding your SSN, guide it jealously like you would protect your most prized possessions. Getting a job, a rental apartment, applying for a loan or other financial services, getting a driver's license, virtually everything is tied to your SSN. So, I cannot emphasize enough that it is your most important identity in America. Beware of fraudsters (through online, phone, email, postal mail, and even physical contact); if fraudsters get a hold of your SSN, full names, date of birth, address and other personal information, they can do lot of damage to you financially, and mess up your credit. And trust me, you don't want that happening to you. So, I would advise you to shred and securely discard documents, letters, etc. containing personal information to avert financial woe. Additional information about the SSN and card can be found on the official website of the social security administration.

2. Get a place to live and get a phone. I think this should be number one on the list of things you need to do as a matter of urgency. But this is subjective.

   Rent a one, two, or three-bedroom apartment, flat or house depending on your unique situation. You may need a family member or friend to guide you in this process and engage the services of an estate agent. Most of the landlords/agents would request for a proof of income, Identification Card, international passport, documentation or immigration papers, and a co-signer. If you do not meet all these requirements, you may suggest to the landlord that you would make upfront payment on your lease term, which Is usually for about 12months. Try and negotiate a deal if possible, that is if you have the cash.

   If you cannot afford to rent just yet, you can live with family and/or friends, on a temporary basis, maybe a week to 2 months depending on your unique situation and the understanding between you and your host family. Please be very sensitive to not inconveniencing your host and becoming a nuisance during this period. You could make small gestures like offering to contribute to grocery expenses, or towards the light bill or other bills. Don't forget to turn off the lights or faucet when not in use. And be clean and tidy. I am pretty sure your host would appreciate these gestures, or they could just tell you not to bother. During this temporary living state, get your SSN, driver's license and a job.

   If you do not have friends/family to live with, you can rent a room on a daily/weekly basis from some cheap hotels that offer this service. Weekly rates are probably cheaper.

   If you are short on cash, you can approach charity, and religious organizations for temporary accommodation assistance. Most of them are happy to assist.

   You can find links to accommodation/rentals/hotel/charity organizations in the housing and accommodation section below.

Also, very important, get a phone, and an email address, so that you can communicate with people easily. You would sometimes want to make inquiries by phone, it's so much easier than walk-ins. Most applications for jobs, houses, or for whatever require a telephone number for call backs. The email address is not as important as the phone number. People will want to talk to you on phone, most 1st and 2nd job interviews are done by phone. And I would suggest you go for telephone carriers with cheap and fixed rates, for example *MetroPCS, Cricket wireless, Tracfone* etc. so that you know exactly how much you're paying every month. *AT&T, Verizon* have great services, but their bills vary monthly, and often you might receive monthly bills that would make you scratch your head.

3. Get a job as soon as possible, because you've got to start earning income, so you can pay your bills, and take care of everyday expenses (depending on your individual circumstance). In addition, being employed is the easiest way to be integrated into the American society, make friends at work, ask questions, learn the way Americans talk, what they mean, what's important to Americans, etc. You may also meet other immigrants at your work site. See *Social integration* section for more ways of integrating into the society.
Links to popular job sites is provided in the *jobs* section below.

# Living in America

## HOUSING AND ACCOMMODATION

We discussed this earlier above, to rent or buy a house check out the following popular rental websites. Of course, there are other websites you could use. Check the websites for 1) Zillow, 2) apartmentguide, 3) apartmentfinder, 4) apartments, and 5) trulia.

For whatever reason my publisher would not approve me writing out the website addresses involved, so for these and other references, just google the websites.

Everywhere you turn, you're most likely to see hotels. The more popular hotels with low price rates, extended stay and/or weekly rates include *Super 8, Motel 6, Studio 6, Budget Inn, travel lodge, travel Inn, Red roof*, and so many others. The pricier hotels include *Hilton, Sheraton, Marriot, Westin, Hyatt, Ritz Carlton etc.* Other popular hotels include *Holiday Inn, Fairfield, courtyard by Marriot, Wyndham, La Quinta Inn.* So many hotels are classified by their star ratings ranging from 1-star to 5-star hotels, depending on the quality and range of services they provide. The choice is yours, there are countless hotels in America.

You can also check out website for Airbnb for your short-term accommodation needs.

You can walk up to the hotels physically or visit their websites to inquire of the services/prices they offer; you can also utilize the following popular websites to compare hotel rates/prices, read customer reviews, and find deals:

1. Kayak
2. priceline
3. trivago
4. tripadvisor
5. hotels

## EDUCATION

If you're a young adult, get a college degree, if you don't have one, (and notice, I said young adult). Great jobs require a college degree. Although most jobs require a high school degree or some work experience, or no work experience, depends. By college degree, I mean a university undergraduate (bachelors) degree. That's another thing, in America, college equates to university, high school equates to secondary school, kindergarten and elementary schools equates to Nursery and primary schools. And then you've got the post graduate degrees, which refers to the master's degree, PhD etc.

If you have a bachelor's degree, don't bother about the master's degree just yet. I advise that you get a job first, and then after a year or two, decide if you need a master's degree for career enhancement, and promotions. The reason being that, if you rush to get a master's degree, you may get a job that does not require a master's degree or even a bachelor's degree, but then you are stuck with a student loan, that you must repay. Student loan debt is real, and it hangs over you like a dark cloud.

By the way, that's from personal experience. Yes, it happened to me. True story, when I was leaving Nigeria in 2008, I had just started my MBA program in Nigeria, and I had at least 15 years of banking experience. I felt good with my career prospects; so naturally when I got to the USA, I wanted to work in a bank, or a financial institution at least. So, after applying to so many banks in Atlanta, GA and having gone through numerous interviews, I would get *push back* emails like "we found someone more qualified than you", or unfortunately we have gone ahead with a more qualified and experienced candidate". And in my mind, I was like how can that be possible? Lol. I wouldn't give up, so what did I do? Naturally I went back to school to get my MBA, so that I could be more qualified; after two years of "bursting my butt" studying, I got an MBA, with a concentration in student loans (lol, just kidding), I got an MBA, with a concentration in Finance. So, I went back and started applying again for jobs, however this time around I expanded my job search beyond the banking industry, and I would get the same push back emails, and this time they always "thanked me for applying" etc. And I was like you know what? FYA! I figured there was a problem somewhere, and it sure wasn't with me. That was a wakeup call for me, and then my mindset started changing from that of an employee, to that of an entrepreneur. But too late, I'm stuck with an unnecessary student loan.

The best undergraduate degrees in America in my opinion, are those in the healthcare, information technology, law, finance, and accounting fields. There are tons of high paying jobs in these industries.

The whole essence of getting a college degree is so you can get a good job, right? And a college degree comes along with student loans, unless you can foot the bill yourself, right? Well good news, there are tons of high paying jobs that don't require a college degree. Concerning education, my candid advice is to learn a thriving trade that's in high demand because there are a few skilled workers, (aviation mechanics, HVAC repair, truck driving, road construction worker, house construction worker, other constructions, car mechanic, etc.), get a certification, or a trade license and begin to earn serious money, save and start your own business. Examples of high paying trades include:

1. Medical Laboratory technician/Dental hygienist
2. Non-commercial Airline pilot/Aircraft mechanic
3. Network Systems Administrator/Database Administrator/Computer programmer
4. HVAC technician
5. Plumber/Electrician/Electrical technician
6. CDL driver
7. Heavy equipment operator
8. Graphic designer
9. Mechanical engineer/technician

Get paid big time, for what you enjoy doing, not what you have to do. These trades require two years or less of training. However, as you progress and gain experience, you will require specific trade certifications, and pass trade examinations, or acquire higher degrees for a highly rewarding career.

One thing I know is, you cannot attain financial freedom from paid employment (except you're the CEO, or President, or an executive of a corporation), you can however attain financial freedom by being a business owner, or an investor. With paid employment, you'll pay your bills, and meet other financial obligations, cool. The same goes for being self-employed. I repeat, the way out of the "rat, or hamster race" is by being a business owner (of proven systems), or an investor, period. The goal should be to have multiple sources of abundant residual income, and have money working hard for you, instead of remaining physically present at a job or business and working hard for money. I usually charge $100 per hour for such financial advice, but for you, my friend, it's free. Lol.

## JOBS AND EMPLOYMENT

The unemployment rate is low right now at 3.9% according to the bureau of labor statistics (2018). You can get a job by walking up to a business and asking if they have any job openings or go online and do a job search on the many job sites available. A few of the most popular job sites include:

1. jobrecruiter
2. indeed
3. monster
4. linkedin
5. craigslist

You can also apply directly to the websites of companies or organizations you are interested in. A lot of these companies with openings would require you to apply online, and there would be follow up interviews, and eventually employment if selected. The turnaround time from application to employment is usually between 2 weeks to 8 weeks. However, you may be able to find instant odd jobs on craigslist's website, or in small sized local neighborhood stores and businesses. For example, the local car wash, or local grocery store, or local bar/restaurant, and a host of other small sized local businesses.

This country is a leveler (my wife always says). What does she mean by that? You must be prepared to roll up your sleeves and work. America does not care if you were a king, or Queen, or Chief executive officer in your country; your foreign work experience, in most cases does not count (with very little exceptions). In most cases, you would be hired for entry level positions. Even if you were a professional with relevant job experience, for example a medical doctor, you would still be required in USA to sit for, and pass the medical board examinations, and it is the same for a lot of other highly skilled professions e.g. nurses, lawyers, dentists etc.

Like I said before, most jobs require a high school diploma for entry positions. However, the following qualities (not exclusive) would work in your favor all the time:

1. Be hardworking
2. Be honest, and dependable
3. Be time conscious (punctual, on time, never late to work)
4. Be coachable (put all you know aside, listen, and learn the required skills necessary to do a great job)
5. Be a problem solver
6. Volunteer to do more (if necessary)
7. Go the extra mile (if required)
8. Do not give excuses
9. Have a "I can do it" and winning mentality
10. Get job specific training/education, and get better in doing your job

## TRANSPORTATION

There are 6 ways of moving around in the USA:
1) *Public transportation, 2) Private transportation, 3) Rideshare, 4)* Car rental, 5) Asking your friend or family relative to take you to your destination all the time, and 6) Walking

We will discuss 1,2, & 3 in this book. 4, 5 & 6 are self-explanatory. Lol, good luck with number 5.

1. *Public Transportation:*

Depending on the town/city you reside, if the transportation service provided by taxi, bus and train is effective and efficient, that's a safe bet for daily transportation.

2. *Private Transportation:*

However, in some other cities it is best to have your own vehicle for daily commute. Which means you've got to go buy and own your vehicle. You can buy cheap used cars for starters on craigslist's website or from your local car shop dealer.

And, of course you'll need to have a driver license before you can drive yourself around. If you have not been issued a USA State driver license, you can still use a valid international driver license for up to one year after your date of entry into the USA, while you are awaiting the issuance of a USA State driver license. However, you'll need to confirm specific requirements from your state DMV (Department of Motor Vehicle).

Also, it is very important to familiarize yourself with the traffic rules here in America before you start driving. Speed limits are in miles (m), not Kilometers (Km), obey all traffic signs and rules always, yield (give way) to and be very careful with pedestrians, cyclists, and motorbikes. All these require some getting used to, I know.

The first time I started driving in Atlanta, when I saw and felt the beautiful roads, especially the highways, (no pot holes, well maintained), wide, and long like an airport tarmac, I was like "wow, these roads would be good for speeding", but then I was quickly cautioned that if I even as go as much one mile over the speed limit, I risk getting an expensive speeding ticket, I was like "dang it, what a waste of good roads". Lol.

True story, a friend of mine who had just come to America, was pulled over by a police patrol car, and he didn't even know he was being pulled over. He said he just noticed this police car behind him with the flashing emergency lights and was wondering to himself "what is going on here?", he didn't know what was happening and so he kept driving slowly until he got home. To cut long story short, he got an expensive ticket for a traffic offense he committed earlier, and for not pulling over when he was told to pull over.

Moral of story is, if a police patrol car is behind you with a flashing emergency light, this means "PULL OVER NOW". What to do? pull over as soon as possible, and as soon as it is safe to do so, pull over to the side of the road, as far to the right side of the road as possible (so that the officer can approach you safely), roll down your window, if it's dark (put on your interior light) put your hands on steering, be calm, and wait for the police officer to come to your car. Do not come out of your vehicle unless instructed by the police officer.

So, what I am saying is if you decide to drive your own vehicle for transportation, pay close attention to the traffic rules and other regulations as provided in the driving lessons and tests at the DMV.

Car purchase options:

Cash: Safe bet is purchase with cash, for a dependable vehicle, sale prices start from $1500 and up. If the vehicle costs less than $1500, it probably would not be dependable, and may have frequent mechanical faults. You do not want this happening to you on the highways of America. If this happens, you'll have to engage the services of a tow company, and they'll charge you fees, and then comes cost of repairs. These can easily rack up to a couple of $100s. So, advice here is invest in a dependable vehicle.

Car Financing: If for whatever reason, you decide to go with car financing, the sale price for the same car, is higher basically because of seller's margin, interest rates and other fees, and you are stuck with a monthly car note payment until paid off.

With financing, after credit approval, you will have to make a down payment of between $100 to whatever you can afford or is required your choice of vehicle. After that, you will be required to make monthly car note payments, which range from $300 to $900, depending on your choice of vehicle. Obviously the higher the cost of the vehicle the higher the monthly car note payment.

3. *Rideshare:*

Alternatively, you can download rideshare apps, and sign up with them. The most popular rideshare apps in America are Uber, and Lyft. You can download both apps on your phone, so you can compare prices and service before you request a ride. First time riders can get free rides depending on city location, using the promo codes below.

For a first time Uber rider, sign up to ride with Uber on their official website, same goes for Lyft. Promocode to sign up for uber, you can use b97gx.

The rideshare companies usually require you to sign up with a credit card, or a debit card. This is because ride fares are charged directly to your card, being a cashless transaction. You would have to download their apps on your phone for easy use after signing up.

**HEALTH INSURANCE**

Hopefully the company you work will provide health insurance (among other benefits) to cover you, and your family, if not sign up for affordable health care on the official website of government healthcare, or request health benefits and assistance from your local county. Alternatively, you can pay out of pocket (cash) for a doctor visit, however this option is usually expensive; Health care cost in America is ridiculously expensive which is why having health insurance coverage is important. For health emergencies, call 911 for medical assistance, or go to the nearest emergency clinic, or ER unit of the nearest hospital.

## FINANCE AND CREDIT

Let's talk finance, (money, money, money). The American economy is a capitalist economy, and there is a lot of financial business transaction going on, every second, and it is going to affect your life in America, one way or another, so it's good you understand how it works, or at least have a basic knowledge of the industry and how the "dice is rolled." Lol. Keeping your head above the "financial" waters is not that hard, if you understand the basics.

A) Credit Bureau:
There are 3 major credit bureaus, Equifax, Transunion, and Experian. They monitor your financial life (bill payment, income, late payment, default in payment, loans granted, loans paid back, credit cards opened etc.) and based on this, they make a report about your credit worthiness. Then they give you a score ranging from 300 (lowest) to 850 (highest). The credit score is a number reflecting the information in your credit report.

If you want to buy a car, rent/buy a house, get a job, or even open a bank account, the first thing these companies or lenders would do (with your permission of course) is request for your credit report/score. Approval/disapproval decisions are mostly based on your credit score and what you have in your report, this presumably helps them determine your ability to pay back any loan they extend to you. A lower credit score indicates to the lenders that you will have challenges paying back any loan or credit extended to you. And a higher credit score indicates that you would most likely not default in loan repayments.

Credit lenders all require a good credit report and score; mostly from 620 and up. Credit scores are classified as follows: Very poor credit is 300 – 579, Fair credit is 580 – 669, Good credit is 670 – 739, Very good credit is 740 – 799, and

Exceptional credit is 800 -850. However, most credit scores for average Americans fall between 600 & 750.

Like I said before, just like your SSN, your credit report/credit score is most important. Guard and monitor it with your life. You might get a break in the first year because at this point, you have little or no credit history, but the first few years are the ones you need to use to discipline yourself and develop a strategy to be on top of your finances. These are the years people make bad financial moves, and unknowingly mess up their credit. Once your credit is messed up, you're toast. Lol.

The secret to good credit, is 1) pay your monthly bills always, 2) pay your bills on time and avoid late payments, 3) avoid owing companies, 4) use cash, or debit card for transactions 5) make monthly payments on your credit cards, 6) keep your credit card balance low, and 7) make or earn more than enough income to cover your monthly expenses.

There are a couple of credit monitoring apps, you can use to check, and monitor your credit. Apps like Experian, myTransunion, Turbo, creditwise, Lifelock, Lexington Law, myFICO, but my favorite is Credit Karma.

B) Inflation and Interest rates
Inflation is mostly defined as the general upward movement of prices of goods and services in an economy or a country. The inflation rate in the USA fell to 2.7% in August 2018 from 2.9% in July 2018, according to tradingeconomics.com

So, what this means is that prices of goods and services, for instance groceries, increase at a rate of 2.7% per year. For example, if a gallon of milk is $1.50 today, all things being equal according to the inflation rate, the gallon of milk would be $1.54 by this time next year. Not bad.

Interest rate is generally the rate at which credit is extended, or what banks charge you when they give you a loan, or the rate of return on an investment. And mind you, this is my own broad uncomplicated definition of the interest rate. This is called the nominal interest rate. The lenders call them many names, for example mortgage rate, lease rate etc. so, when you borrow money from the bank, in form of a mortgage, auto or personal loan, you will pay back the interest charged in addition to the principal amount of the loan.

However, the lenders complicate this simple process with what they call an APR (annual percentage rate) where they confuse you, lol, but it's all good. In an APR, they include fees, charges and consider some other variables. The APR is usually slightly higher that the nominal interest rate, and it is usually what the lenders would use in their loan offers. This APR could also be fixed or variable depending. For more information about annual percentage rates, you can visit bank rates website.

The Interest rate is currently in a range of 1.75% to 2% according to a report by The New York Times in August 2018.

So, assuming you finance your new car with an auto loan of $20,000 with an interest rate of 2%, to payback in 1 year; you should pay back $20,400 at the end of 1 year (with monthly payments of $1,700). This is the easiest calculation of an interest rate. But like I said earlier, the lenders use the APR (which is a higher rate, and depends on your credit score), and pay back is usually longer than one year. This is good information, yes? Cool.

C) The stock exchange markets
All companies are divided into public or private companies. The public companies trade their shares in the stock exchange market. So, the stock exchange market is a market where the shares or stocks of public companies are exchanged or traded. For example, the shares of Ford motors, Facebook, Apple, Amazon, and a lot of other companies are sold and bought by the public in the stock exchange market.

The value of a company is simply the price of the stock of the company multiplied by the number of paid shareholders of the company. Now, the share prices of these companies fluctuate by the second, by the minute, by the hour, and daily, depending on a whole lot of factors. The value of these public companies is never the same. It changes rapidly, even in a day. This fluctuation is called stock volatility, and results in a lot speculating in the movement of the prices of these stocks by some stock traders or investors.

People make money, and people lose money in the stock market. Anybody interested in the shares of these companies can buy them through a licensed stock broker. The three major U.S. stock exchange markets include, The New York Stock Exchange Market (The NYSE), The National Association of Securities Dealers Automated Quotation System (The NASDAQ), and The American Stock Exchange (The AMEX).

D) The USA Currency

The official currency of USA is the US Dollar and cents. I know you know this already, however what is important here is to know the name of the coins because people refer to them in their conversations often, and for you to know how many of these different coins make one US Dollar. In addition, when you go to the gas station, or the grocery store, you might pay with cash, and receive change in coins. So, it is good to know your coins, and the various denominations of the Dollar bill. Money is a language everybody understands.

|   | Cents | Name of Coins | How many cents make 1 Dollar |
|---|-------|---------------|------------------------------|
| 1 | 0.01  | Penny         | 100                          |
| 2 | 0.05  | Nickel        | 20                           |
| 3 | 0.10  | Dime          | 10                           |
| 4 | 0.25  | Quarter       | 4                            |
| 5 | 0.50  | Half Dollar   | 2                            |

The coins also include the $1 coin.

The denominations of the US Dollar Note include the following: $1 bill, $2 bill, $5 bill, $10 bill, $20 bill, $50 bill, and the $100 bill.

## TAXES

It is very important that you file your taxes yearly with the Inland Revenue Service (IRS). Taxes are a major source of revenue for the government and helps pay for the cost of providing social and economic amenities, and costs of running some other business of government.

The time to file your taxes is usually between January to April of the year following the year you want to file your taxes for. For example, you file taxes for the year 2018, between January and April 2019. The IRS would normally let us know when the deadline is to file our taxes.

You can file your tax for free on the official website of the IRS, all other tax info can also be obtained on this same website.

## SEX & MARRIAGE

If he or she says No, it's a No, not maybe; stop the play immediately, chill out, and try again some other time, or look for someone else. If not, you could be accused of rape, and you'll go to jail, and then you're messed up.

Don't get anyone pregnant, if you do not plan to marry her. If you do, you'll be paying child support for a long time (until the child becomes 18 years old) enforced by the court of law. Your wages, or paycheck could be garnished, meaning the government will take money directly from you your paycheck and pay child support to the woman involved. And you'll have little or no money for yourself. The American woman would not abort her unborn baby because you as a man are not ready for a child. Most of the time she has the resources and support to take care of her baby. Most abortions take place for health reasons. Your American girlfriend would not just have an abortion just because you ask her to. So, if you not ready to start a family, use contraception.

Court your boyfriend or girlfriend for a while to determine if you're right each other, fall in love and get married. If you rush in, I assure you, you'll rush out. Even though Americans love and respect the marriage institution, they have no qualms about getting a divorce, it's like they do not think twice about the consequences. If they're not comfortable with the marriage arrangement, they'll be out, in a minute. No wonder there are so many divorce lawyers in America, it's big business. And your partner will be entitled to half of all you own, aside from child support. And this would be enforced by the courts. So, my friend be certain and sure you're ready before you get married.

## RULES AND LAWS

This is a country of laws. If you break the law, you will be prosecuted, and could go to jail, or pay a fine or both.

There is no begging, or pleading with law enforcement officers in America, unlike the countries we emigrated from, right? In America, you break the law, you'll be caught, and you'll be brought to book. That is why, everything seems to work here because everyone is aware of and obey the rules and laws of the land. Probably in your country you can talk, plead, or bribe your way out of a situation, here that doesn't happen. If you try it, you've just committed another offense. The thought won't even cross your mind. Security of life and property is top priority. There are cameras everywhere, citizens call 911 to report crimes, or to prevent a possible crime, and when you see the police patrol car, speeding by, and flashing their lights, they're responding to a criminal emergency and they going to get someone. The policemen and policewomen here don't play. Some of them look like robot cops, well I know they do in Atlanta; compare them to the images of the cops you have in your country, lol. See what I mean? The policemen in your home country, some of them probably have pot bellies, and are physically out of shape. Or they are ill equipped with obsolete weapons and/or lack forensic science to fight crime.

In America, nobody is above the law, not even the president of the USA and everyone is equal in the eyes of justice. The blindfold on the lady justice here in America is tightly in place, the blindfold is not loose, nor is she peeping (as in some other countries). So, do not be afraid, be kind and honest, be hardworking, obey the traffic laws, do not break any law of the land, and stay out of trouble. You'll be alright.

### THE AMERICAN FLAG, the National Anthem and the Pledge of allegiance

The American Flag has 50 stars representing the 50 states of the United States, and the red and white stripes represent the 13 original colonies.

(Picture of flag courtesy of newstarget.com)

The national anthem is often referred to as the "The star-spangled banner", and it is a song about the American flag, written in 1814 by Francis Scott King.

## The National Anthem/The Star-spangled banner:

O say can you see by the dawn's early light,

What so proudly we hailed at the twilight's last gleaming,

Whose broad stripes and bright stars through the perilous fight,

O'er the ramparts we watched, were so gallantly streaming?

And the rockets' red glare, the bombs bursting in the air,

Gave proof through the night that our flag was still there;

O say does that star-spangled banner yet wave,

O'er the land of the free and home of the brave?


## The Pledge:

"I pledge allegiance to the flag of the United States of America,

and to the Republic for which it stands,

one nation under God,

indivisible with liberty and justice for all".


## POLITICS AND GOVERNMENT

There are two major political parties in the USA; the Republican party, and the Democratic party. The government of the USA is made up of three equal branches, the Executive, Legislative, and the Judiciary branches.

The Executive branch enforces laws and is led by the President of the United States. The current president is Mr. Donald J. Trump.

The Legislative branch, also known as the congress make laws, and comprises of

i)   the **House of Representatives** led by the Speaker of the House. The current speaker of the House is Nancy Pelosi,

ii)  the **Senate** led by the Senate Majority Leader. The current Senate Majority Leader is Mitch McConnell

The Judiciary branch interprets laws and the constitution; It is a system of courts and judges. The Judiciary is led by the nine Justices of the Supreme Court. The Supreme court is the highest court of the land.

The 50 state governments are led by the various state governors, the members of the state legislatures, and the various judges of the state courts. Every city has a Mayor, and a city council.

*50 States:*

There are 50 states in the United States of America. In addition, there are 5 major United States territories: American Samoa, The U.S. Virgin Islands, Puerto Rico, Guam, and the Northern Mariana Islands. It is important to note that the U.S. territories are not U.S. states, however the people are U.S. citizens except for the people of American Samoa, who are U.S. nationals.

The 50 States of America include the following:

|   | STATE | CAPITAL |
|---|-------|---------|
| 1 | Alabama (AL) | Montgomery |
| 2 | Alaska (AK) | Juneau |
| 3 | Arizona (AZ) | Phoenix |
| 4 | Arkansas (AR) | Little Rock |
| 5 | California (CA) | Sacramento |
| 6 | Colorado (CO) | Denver |
| 7 | Connecticut (CT) | Hartford |
| 8 | Delaware (DE) | Dover |
| 9 | Florida (FL) | Tallahassee |
| 10 | Georgia (GA) | Atlanta |
| 11 | Hawaii (HI) | Honolulu |
| 12 | Idaho (ID) | Boise |
| 13 | Illinois (IL) | Springfield |

| | | |
|---|---|---|
| 14 | Indiana (IN) | Indianapolis |
| 15 | Iowa (IA) | Des Moines |
| 16 | Kansas (KS) | Topeka |
| 17 | Kentucky (KY) | Frankfort |
| 18 | Louisiana (LA) | Baton Rouge |
| 19 | Maine (ME) | Augusta |
| 20 | Maryland (MD) | Annapolis |
| 21 | Massachusetts (MA) | Boston |
| 22 | Michigan (MI) | Lansing |
| 23 | Minnesota (MN) | St Paul |
| 24 | Mississippi (MS) | Jackson |
| 25 | Missouri (MO) | Jefferson City |
| 26 | Montana (MT) | Helena |
| 27 | Nebraska (NE) | Lincoln |
| 28 | Nevada (NV) | Carson City |
| 29 | New Hampshire (NH) | Concord |
| 30 | New Jersey (NJ) | Trenton |
| 31 | New Mexico (NM) | Santa Fe |
| 32 | New York (NY) | Albany |
| 33 | North Carolina (NC) | Raleigh |
| 34 | North Dakota (ND) | Bismarck |
| 35 | Ohio (OH) | Columbus |
| 36 | Oklahoma (OK) | Oklahoma City |
| 37 | Oregon (OR) | Salem |
| 38 | Pennsylvania (PA) | Harrisburg |
| 39 | Rhode Island (RI) | Providence |
| 40 | South Carolina (SC) | Columbia |
| 41 | South Dakota (SD) | Pierre |
| 42 | Tennessee (TN) | Nashville |
| 43 | Texas (TX) | Austin |
| 44 | Utah (UT) | Salt Lake City |
| 45 | Vermont (VT) | Montpelier |
| 46 | Virginia (VA) | Richmond |
| 47 | Washington (WA) | Olympia |
| 48 | West Virginia (WV) | Charleston |
| 49 | Wisconsin (WI) | Madison |
| 50 | Wyoming (WY) | Cheyenne |

MAP SHOWING THE 50 STATES OF USA:

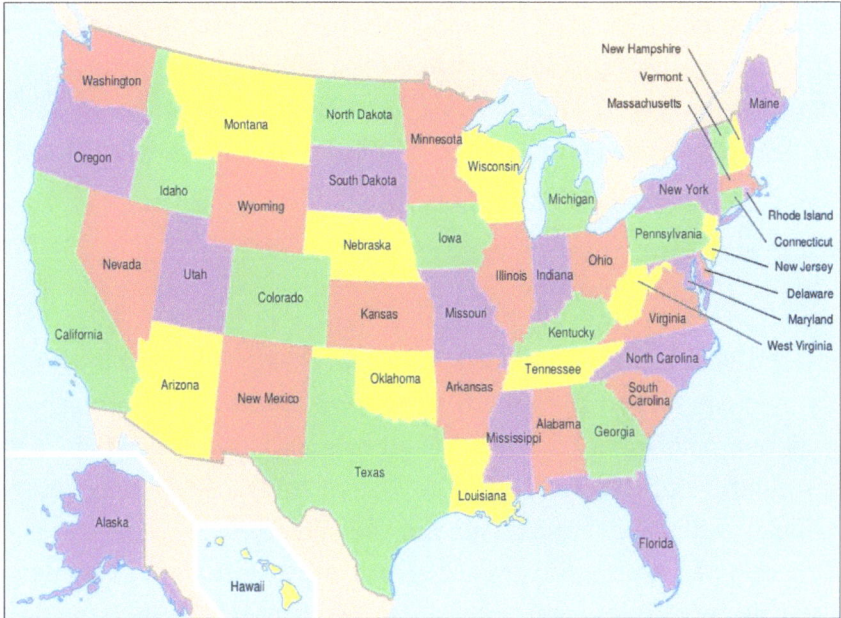

(Map courtesy of Wikipedia commons)

## Counties:

We also have what is called counties; this is the equivalent of a local government in most other countries. A county may comprise of a city, several cities, towns and rural developments. So, each state in the USA, comprises of several counties. The counties exist so that the various services of government can be accessible to the citizens in their local areas. The state with the lowest number of counties is Delaware, which has 3 counties, while the state with the largest number of counties is Texas, which has 254 counties.

A county has its own government (with elected county commissioners) which however is subordinate to the state government. Major responsibilities of a county include public education management, maintenance of public utilities, and law enforcement; So, it is not uncommon to have a county police, in addition to a state police.

*Voting rights:*

Every citizen aged 18 years old, and older has the right to vote in an election. Permanent residents, green card holders, and all other immigrants, or visitors cannot vote. Only citizens can vote. This is the major difference between a green card holder, and a citizen; the right to vote.

## POPULATION AND DEMOGRAPHICS

Immigration is not a new concept in America, in fact the United States of America was founded by early immigrants from Europe in the early 1600s, and since then the country has seen an influx of immigrants from all over the world. So be comfortable and assured in this fact. The population of USA is 328,054,892 as at July 4, 2018, according to the official website of the census bureau. The website also states that there is one new immigrant every 28 seconds, that is mind blowing (wow)! The table below shows the highest populated state to the lowest populated state in the USA.

| Rank | State | Population |
|------|-------|-----------|
| 1 | California | 39,536,653 |
| 2 | Texas | 28,304,596 |
| 3 | Florida | 20,984,400 |
| 4 | New York | 19,849,399 |
| 5 | Pennsylvania | 12,805,537 |
| 6 | Illinois | 12,802,023 |
| 7 | Ohio | 11,658,609 |
| 8 | Georgia | 10,429,379 |
| 9 | North Carolina | 10,273,419 |
| 10 | Michigan | 9,962,311 |
| 11 | New Jersey | 9,005,644 |
| 12 | Virginia | 8,470,020 |
| 13 | Washington | 7,405,743 |
| 14 | Arizona | 7,016,270 |
| 15 | Massachusetts | 6,859,819 |
| 16 | Tennessee | 6,715,984 |

| | | |
|---|---|---|
| 17 | Indiana | 6,666,818 |
| 18 | Missouri | 6,113,532 |
| 19 | Maryland | 6,052,177 |
| 20 | Wisconsin | 5,795,483 |
| 21 | Colorado | 5,607,154 |
| 22 | Minnesota | 5,576,606 |
| 23 | South Carolina | 5,024,369 |
| 24 | Alabama | 4,874,747 |
| 25 | Louisiana | 4,684,333 |
| 26 | Kentucky | 4,454,189 |
| 27 | Oregon | 4,142,776 |
| 28 | Oklahoma | 3,930,864 |
| 29 | Connecticut | 3,588,184 |
| 30 | Iowa | 3,145,711 |
| 31 | Utah | 3,101,833 |
| 32 | Arkansas | 3,004,279 |
| 33 | Nevada | 2,998,039 |
| 34 | Mississippi | 2,984,100 |
| 35 | Kansas | 2,913,123 |
| 36 | New Mexico | 2,088,070 |
| 37 | Nebraska | 1,920,076 |
| 38 | West Virginia | 1,815,857 |
| 39 | Idaho | 1,716,943 |
| 40 | Hawaii | 1,427,538 |
| 41 | New Hampshire | 1,342,795 |
| 42 | Maine | 1,335,907 |
| 43 | Rhode Island | 1,059,639 |
| 44 | Montana | 1,050,493 |
| 45 | Delaware | 961,939 |
| 46 | South Dakota | 869,666 |
| 47 | North Dakota | 755,393 |
| 48 | Alaska | 739,795 |
| 49 | Vermont | 623,657 |
| 50 | Wyoming | 579,315 |

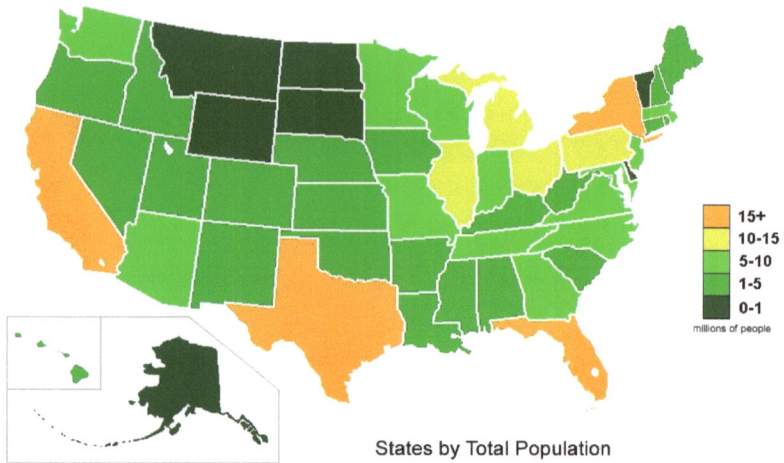

States by Total Population

(Map courtesy of Wikipedia commons)

The demographics, of the USA population consists of people from almost all races of the world. This singular factor makes USA a unique country.

| Race | Percentage |
| --- | --- |
| White alone (not Hispanic or Latino) | 60.7% |
| Hispanic or Latino | 18.1% |
| Black (African American) alone | 13.4% |
| American Indian, Alaska Native alone | 1.3% |
| Asian alone | 5.8% |
| Native Hawaiian/Pacific Islanders alone | 0.2% |
| Two or more races | 2.7% |

(Courtesy of US Census Bureau)

## MOST POPULAR SPORTS, & LEAGUES

Just like much of the world, sports are a big part of American culture, and sports followership is something of a pop culture in the USA. Most major cities have big league teams, and huge sports fan support.

The most popular sports, and most prominent leagues, or associations in the USA are: American football, basketball, baseball, soccer, ice hockey, car racing, tennis, golf, MMA and boxing. I mean, there are other sports however these are the major ones.

| SPORTS | LEAGUE |
|---|---|
| American Football | National football League (NFL) |
| Baseball | Major League Baseball (MLB) |
| Basketball | National Basketball Association (NBA) |
| Ice Hockey | National hockey League (NHL) |
| Soccer | Major League Soccer (MLS) |
| Boxing | WBA, WBC, IBF, WBO |
| Auto Racing | NASCAR, INDYCAR |
| Golf | USGA, PGA |
| Tennis | US Tennis Association (UTSA) |
| Mixed Martial Arts (MMA) | Ultimate Fighting Championship (UFC) |

## NATIONAL HOLIDAYS

The national holidays in the USA include:

| New Year's Day | January 1 |
|---|---|
| Inauguration Day | January 20 |
| Martin Luther King's Day | 3rd Monday in January |
| George Washington's Birthday | 3rd Monday in February |
| Memorial Day | Last Monday in May |
| Independence Day | July 4 |
| Labor Day | 1st Monday in September |
| Columbus Day | 2nd Monday in October |
| Veterans Day | November 11 |
| Thanksgiving Day | 4th Thursday in November |
| Christmas Day | December 25 |

## SOCIAL INTEGRATION

According to Wikipedia, Social integration "is the process during which newcomers or minorities are incorporated into the social structure of the host society." Let me give you another definition of social integration, according to the website of migrationpolicy, "Immigrant integration is the process by which immigrants and their children come to feel and become participants in the life of their country of destination, and in its schools, workplaces, and communities." (both extracted 09/12/2018).

I am not going to bother myself with the definitions, lol; I will just say that an immigrant can be integrated into America through a variety of ways, the most common from my experience are the following:

1. **Associations**
   I play a lot of tennis for recreational and exercise purposes, so when I newly came to America, one of the first things I looked for was a tennis court, and I found one in a park near my house. I started playing and in a short time, I had become friends with some other tennis players; we would have occasional events like cook outs, birthday parties, mini competitions, exchange ideas and engage in a host of social discussions, and this helped integrate me into the society. A lot of them are still my friends today. This might work for you too. You can join professional associations and attend meetings, and become active in their monthly or annual activities, you can make friends in your place of worship, and you can join local business associations, or chamber of commerce.

2. **Job/school**
   When you attend a school, or in your work place, you will meet different people that you will interact with daily, and learn about work ethics, and social expectations as it pertains to behavioral attitudes.

3. **Volunteering/Attending network events**
   You can join volunteer groups if you have the time to donate your time and skills to benefit your immediate neighborhood for free. Business, professional, and social networking events

are also a good place to meet people and exchange ideas and get to know people better.

4. **Internet/Television/Radio**
   A lot of information is available on television, and by watching some TV, or cable programs you can learn a lot about the American culture, her people, how they live, and what's important to them. Programs like Modern Family, The Simpsons, Blackish, Saturday Night live, the tonight show, NCIS, Law & Order, Andy Griffith Show, Cosby Show, Roseanne, all in the Family etc., there are a lot of them. Listening to news programs in the media will inform you about current events in the social and political scene, on both the national level and in your local environment. You check out CNN, FOX News, Good morning America, The View etc. Local TV stations are also very good for receiving information concerning your immediate locality. Listening to American music is also a very good source of gaining insight about the American culture.

With the above activities, you would learn a lot about the social character, and the culture of the American people; and how to blend into the society.

**LANGUAGE AND PRONUNCIATION**

The official language of America is English, the Spanish language is fast becoming a 2nd language in some states, especially in the southern states of Texas, Arizona, California, and maybe Georgia? Hopefully you understand the English language, this helps for quick integration. If you do not understand the English language, it's not a big problem, you're not alone, there are millions of immigrants and citizens who do not have a perfect command of the English language.

However, what you need to do is learn the English language as fast as you can, anyhow you can, and work on your accent. This is important for communication purposes, of course; there are many resources for learning the English language online, and offline. Physical classes, or online classes. Just google "how to learn English" and you would see numerous resources available to you. While it takes years, maybe decades, and sometimes impossible to eliminate your accent, you can work to minimize the sound of your accent. Eliminating your accent is very difficult because you still speak your native language. Even if you decide foolishly to stop speaking your native language, it's still going to take you a lifetime to eliminate your accent totally.

The challenge with having an accent when speaking English, is some people may find it hard to understand you, even though you are speaking English. Accents especially thick accents distort words spoken, makes imperfect communication sent by you to the recipient. So, for effective verbal communication, speak slowly, increase the tone of your voice (loud, but not too loud) and as clear as you can. Enunciating, and gesticulations with your hands always helps. Also remember to make eye contact when speaking. Not making eye contact may mean you are weak, or lying, or suggest some other negative meaning.

Yes, because with an accent, you are saying something, and the person you are talking to thinks you're saying something else because they can't understand you. And this can be frustrating, repeating yourself like you don't know what you are talking about. You've been speaking English all your life, but now you begin to doubt yourself, and your knowledge of the English language, lol.

You know what's funny? When the American speaks, with an American accent (and they speak fast too, almost like rapping to music, some also speak slowly) you as an immigrant "must" understand what they are saying. You can't say "I can't hear you" or "I don't understand you", you must make extra effort to understand what they are saying. Why? Because they are most likely your boss at your new job, or persons in charge at the other places where you go to get some help or whatever, and you are eager to assimilate, after all, you are the immigrant, the one trying to learn a new culture. I wish this effort was reciprocal, but it's not in a lot of cases.

Some will understand you but still tell you they don't know what you are talking about because they don't want to deal with it. Funny right? No, it's frustrating, very frustrating. However, it is what it is, so be ready for that. My advice? Be yourself, be confident in your knowledge of the English language, speak clearly as much as you can, speak up (loud), and be bold in your skills and abilities. And it is comforting to know that even Americans from the different parts of the country have accents depending on which part of the country they originate from, so you would hear some people talk with say a "Southern accent" "Northern accent", "New York accent", or "Texas accent" etc. So cool.

Also, very important, there is what we call American English and English as we (as immigrants) know it, the English language the rest of the world speaks. In America, you've got a lot of cases where different words are used to name or describe the same thing. Such that when you talking to an American (in English, of course with your accent) he may not understand you because you are using a different word (than what he is used to) in your sentence. For example, if you tell an American "I put the items in the car boot". He'll be confused because in America, a car boot is called a car trunk. He'll be like "what?" "Where?" "Speak English!" And you'll be like "I said in the boot" (confused, starting to feel a little less confident of yourself, and doubting your mastery of the language you've spoken all your life). Here are a few examples:

| UNIVERSAL ENGLISH (UK) | AMERICAN ENGLISH |
| --- | --- |
| Biscuits | Cookies |
| Sweets | Candy |
| Soft drinks | Soda |
| Car bonnet | Hood |
| Car boot | Trunk |
| Brake lights | Tail lights, break lights |
| Head light | Head lamp |
| Indicator | Signal light |
| Fuel / Fuel station | Gas / Gas station |
| Football | Soccer |

| | |
|---|---|
| Lawn tennis | Tennis |
| Supermarket | Grocery Store |
| Shopping Center | Shopping Mall |
| Expressway/Motorway | Highway |
| Jeep | SUV |
| Flats | Apartments |
| Housing estate | Sub division |
| Tissue paper | Napkin |
| Cutlery | Silverware |
| Nursery school | Kindergarten |
| Primary School | Elementary school |
| Secondary/grammar School | High school |
| University | College |
| Pants | Underwear |
| Trousers | Pants |
| Singlet | Undershirt |
| Garage | Parking deck, car lot |
| Military barracks | Military base |
| Reception | Front desk |
| Guest Toilet | Rest room, Bathroom |
| Tap | Faucet |

Reading books, and magazines can help with spelling, and getting yourself familiarized with how Americans spell. Also pay close attention to how words are pronounced by other people around you, or on television, and radio.

Dates too:

Assuming this date, March 4, 2019. Americans will write this date as 03/04/2019, the rest of the world writes the same date as 04/03/2019.

## GEOGRAPHY

The USA is the 3rd largest country in the world after Russia, and China. It is bordered in the north by Canada, in the west by the Pacific Ocean, in the south by Mexico, and the Gulf of Mexico, and to the east by the Atlantic Ocean.

(Map courtesy of landscape)

The five great lakes (Superior, Michigan, Huron, Erie, and Ontario) are located towards the north east, or north central of the country, and forms part of the border with Canada. The Rocky Mountains stretch through the western part of the USA, and the Appalachian Mountains are in the eastern part of the USA. In the middle of the country, we have the great plains, which is a vast expanse of grass lands.

# Köppen climate types of the United States

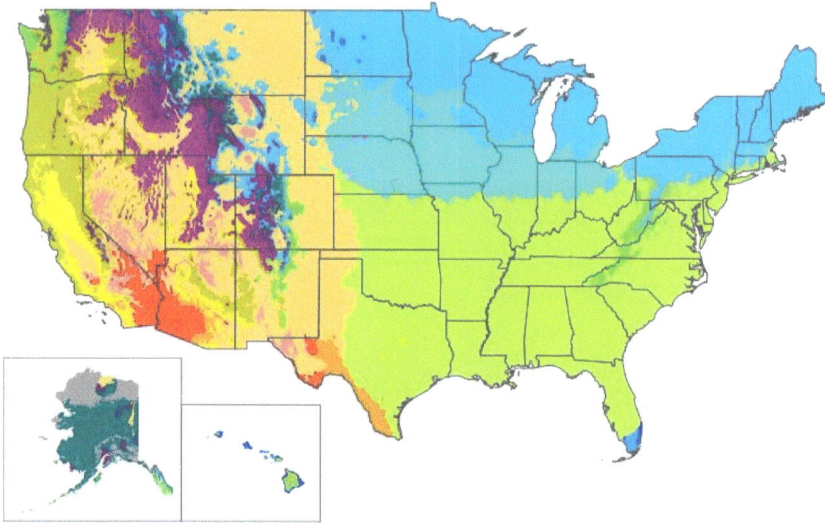

## Köppen climate type

| | | |
|---|---|---|
| EF (Ice-cap) | Dsb (Warm-summer mediterranean continental) | Csa (Hot-summer mediterranean) |
| ET (Tundra) | Dsa (Hot-summer mediterranean continental) | BSk (Cold semi-arid) |
| Dfc (Subarctic) | Cfc (Subpolar oceanic) | BSh (Hot semi-arid) |
| Dfb (Warm-summer humid continental) | Cfb (Oceanic) | BWk (Cold desert) |
| Dfa (Hot-summer humid continental) | Cfa (Humid subtropical) | BWh (Hot desert) |
| Dwc (Subarctic) | Cwb (Subtropical highland) | Aw (Savanna) |
| Dwb (Warm-summer humid continental) | Cwa (Humid subtropical) | Am (Monsoon) |
| Dwa (Hot-summer humid continental) | Csc (Cold-summer mediterranean) | Af (Rainforest) |
| Dsc (Dry-summer subarctic) | Csb (Warm-summer mediterranean) | |

*Isotherm used to distinguish temperate (C) and continental (D) climates is -3°C

Data sources: Köppen types calculated from data from PRISM Climate Group, Oregon State University, http://prism.oregonstate.edu; Outline map from US Census Bureau

(Courtesy of Wikipedia commons)

The USA has almost all the climates of the world; the country is that big. We've got hot arid desert climate, temperate region, tropical dry/wet season, Mediterranean climate, etc. But this climate conditions occur in different parts of the country. Generally, it's colder in the northern part of the country, and it gets warmer as go south.

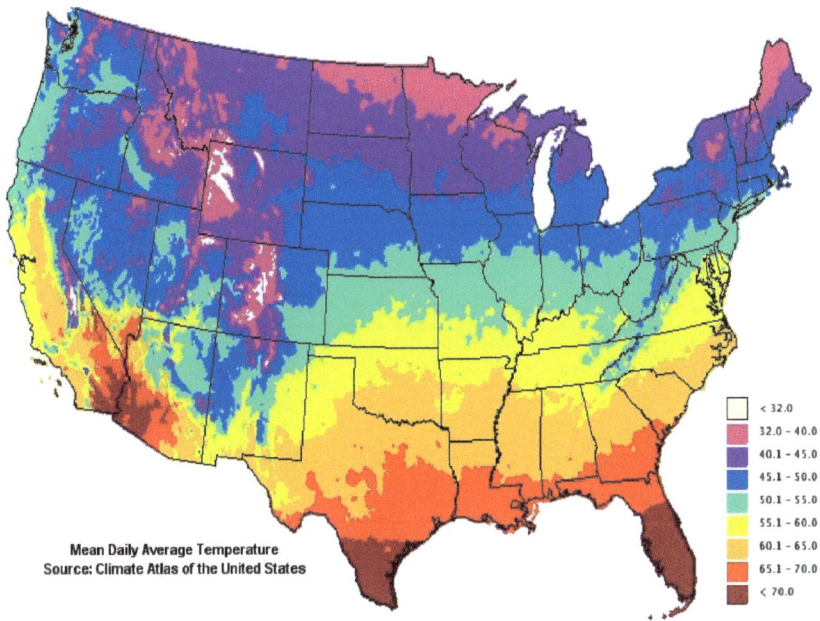

Mean Daily Average Temperature
Source: Climate Atlas of the United States

| | |
|---|---|
| | < 32.0 |
| | 32.0 – 40.0 |
| | 40.1 – 45.0 |
| | 45.1 – 50.0 |
| | 50.1 – 55.0 |
| | 55.1 – 60.0 |
| | 60.1 – 65.0 |
| | 65.1 – 70.0 |
| | < 70.0 |

(Map courtesy of Ducksters)

As shown above the major rivers of the USA include the Columbia, Colorado, Missouri, Mississippi, Hudson, and the Rio Grande. The River Rio Grande forms part of the border with Mexico. The Mississippi river is the longest river in the USA (and the 4th longest in the world).

TIME ZONE MAP of the USA:

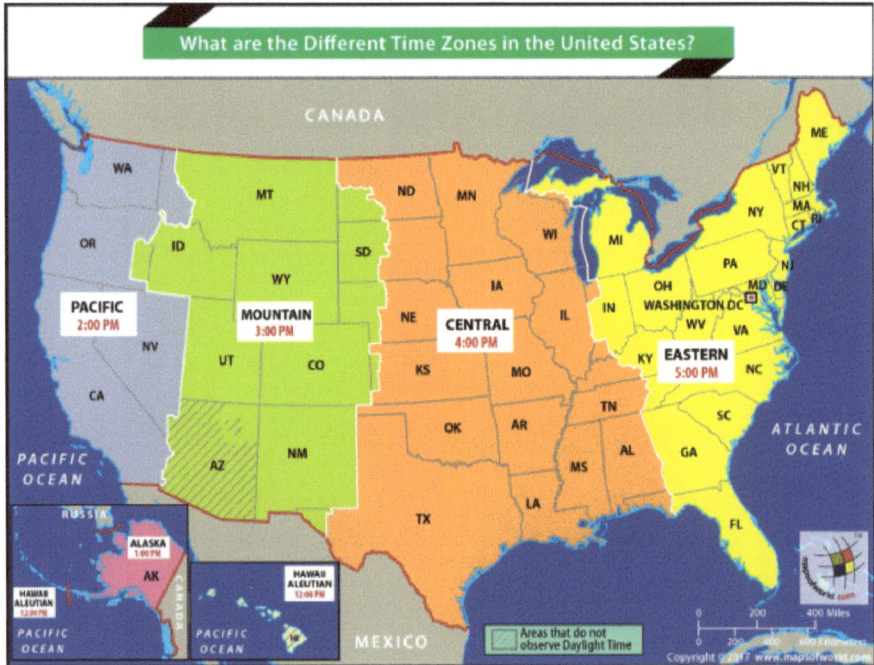

(Map courtesy of Mapsofworld)

The USA has 6 different time zones: Pacific, Mountain, Central, Eastern, Alaska, and Hawaii standard time zones. Therefore, if it's 6pm in the eastern zone (EST), then it would be 5pm CST (Central time), 4pm MST (Mountain time), 3pm PST (Pacific time), 2pm AST (Alaska time) and 1pm HST (Hawaii time).

## MILITARY AND LAW ENFORCEMENT AGENCIES

We Americans love our military men and women, law enforcement officers (Police, State Bureau of Investigations (SBI), and Federal Bureau of Investigations (FBI)), and first responders (firefighters, and emergency workers). These courageous and selfless people keep us safe from bad people (domestic, and foreign), and provide help to us in our most vulnerable times of need. Every chance you get, appreciate and thank them for their selfless service. And truly mean it. Without them America would be like the country you emigrated from. Also, if you feel compelled to serve and you meet the requirements, sign up for service. They are always looking for brave people to recruit and serve the country. And the various agencies have great pay & employment benefits.

So, whereas in most other countries, the various arms of the armed forces consist of the Army, Navy, and Airforce, In USA, they consist of the Army, Navy, Airforce, Marine corps, and the Coast Guard.

## CONCLUSION

I end this book, by wishing you well, and pray that you meet with good fortunes and good success. May your American dreams become reality for you and your family.

God bless you, and may God bless the United States of America, Amen.